AZU's Dreams of Laos
Vientiane

Published in 2007 by
AZU Editions (Thailand) Ltd.
111 SKV Building, 8/Fl
Soi Sansabai, Sukhumvit Soi 36
Klongton, Klongtoey
Bangkok 10110
Thailand

Tel: 66 (0)2 712-4016
Fax: 66 (0)2 661-2894
office@azueditions.com
www.azueditions.com

ISBN 978-974-8136-55-4

Printed in Malaysia

Cover: A cyclist rides past That Luang,
the national symbol of Laos.

AZU'S
DREAMS OF LAOS™

Vientiane

Photographs by Martin Reeves
Text by John Hoskin

AZU

'*Moon City*'
is usually given as the literal

translation of Vientiane, the capital of Laos. Alternatively, depending on one's reading of etymology, the name could mean 'Sandalwood City.' Both are evocative titles that speak of somewhere different, and Vientiane, the smallest and least well-known of Southeast Asian capitals, is a place that defies comparisons.

Much less of a somnolent city than it was just a few years ago, especially in increasing traffic and expanding accommodation and dining options, Vientiane changes at its own chosen pace,

Previous spread:
Vientiane's cityscape remains largely traditional and low-rise.

Left: Even on the city's main boulevards, life, and the traffic, moves at a leisurely pace.

5

seeming to prefer the mantle of a country town rather than that of a budding metropolis.

Away from the main thoroughfares the streets seem more rural than urban, with grass verges, shade trees, and a tranquil air disturbed by little more than a passing bicycle. There is indeed a decided lack of the chaotic bustle that generally typifies Asian cities, and here one can stroll at ease.

Vientiane derives much of its air of peace and tranquility from the Mekong, on the banks of which the town nestles. There is a timelessness to this river, which unlike most of the world's other major waterways, has so far been scarcely touched by man. And therein lies an irony; Vientiane owes its long history to the very fact of the river.

Above left: Pedal power has yet to be totally eclipsed by the internal combustion engine.

Right: Fishing in the shallows of the Mekong River at sunset.

Laos is largely a mountainous country and, thus, the Mekong River has historically been its principal communication link, while its narrow valley has provided the most suitable land for settlements and rice cultivation.

Before the country was unified as the 'Kingdom of a Million Elephants' in the fourteenth century, with Luang Prabang as its capital, Vientiane was the site of just a petty fiefdom. By the sixteenth century, however, it had risen to pre-eminence, superseding the northern city as the kingdom's power base, as well as gaining a reputation as a regional centre of Buddhist learning.

Yet, Vientiane did not long enjoy power or independence. Internal divisions, invasions by the

Above left: Rural scenes are encountered scarcely beyond the city limits.

Right: French colonial influence is most readily apparent in the lasting popularity of French bread.

Siamese, French colonial rule, a US presence during the Vietnam War, and Soviet influence after the communist takeover in 1975 all affected urban development.

Much of the city's allure comes from such an intriguing mix of influences, though none are so dominant as to detract from an individual identity. Even the impact of French colonialism, which left such a stamp on other Indochina cities, such as Saigon (now Ho Chi Minh City) and Phnom Penh, was modest. A few baroque facades and impressive boulevards are only dimly discernable, but what is still noticeable is that the baguette remains as much a staple food as a bowl of rice.

Vientiane's indigenous cultural heritage was severely damaged when the Siamese sacked the

city in 1828, though with a determined survival instinct, the Lao rebuilt the temples that had been destroyed.

Thus, Wat Phra Keo, which was originally constructed in the sixteenth century to enshrine the statue of the Emerald Buddha (now in Bangkok), was faithfully restored in the twentieth century and is now maintained as a museum.

More fortunate was Wat Sisaket. Perhaps because it had only recently been completed at the time of their invasion, the Siamese left it intact to survive today as one of the city's most beautiful and most fascinating temples. Particularly eye-catching are the interior walls of the cloisters, which are studded with niches intended for Buddha images; the fine mural

Above left: In traditional style, the pediment of Wat Phra Keo is richly ornamented.

Right: Niches holding Buddha images line the cloisters of Wat Sisaket.

paintings in the main chapel; and a ceiling decorated with floral designs that were copied from Siamese temples at Ayutthaya, the original inspiration, however, being French.

While Wat Sisaket and Vientiane's other temples display Thai architectural and decorative influences, the city's most sacred shrine, That Luang, is pure Lao. In spite of somewhat formidable surrounding walls and a complex design, That Luang possesses a transcendent beauty in its central stupa. This graceful square structure, decorated with sober mouldings, appears both slender and powerful. Like Vientiane itself, it achieves a marked appeal, all the more surprising for the lack of obvious ornamentation.

Left: Without obvious ornamentation, That Luang still possesses a unique grace and symmetry.

Following spread: The Mekong River, especially at sunset, is a city focal point.

13

Above: A motorcycle can
easily serve all the family.

Right: Although traffic
is increasing, Vientiane
is still less congested than
most Asian capitals.

Left: *Reminiscent of the Arc de Triomphe in Paris, the Patuxai commemorates the Lao who died in pre-revolutionary wars.*

Above: *A statue of King Sisavang Vong, who declared independence from France after World War II.*

19

Previous spread: *According to legend, That Luang enshrines a sacred relic of the Buddha. It stands as a symbol of both Buddhism and Lao sovereignty.*

Left and above: *That Luang's architectural detail complements the simple grace of the central tower.*

23

Left: *Tuk-tuks await passengers as Wat Tad Foun looms in the background.*

Above: *Fresh produce for sale at a small roadside market outside That Luang.*

Above: *Fa Ngum Park presents a mix of statuary and tropical flora.*

Right: *Wat Phra Keo once enshrined the image of the Emerald Buddha.*

Above: Detail of a statue of a Chinese goddess at Chua Bang-Long Temple.

Right: The Chinese temple of Chua Bang-Long is an eclectic mix of architectural and decorative styles.

Following pages (left): A quiet street overshadowed by the top of the Patuxai. *(right):* Monks arriving by tuk-tuk at Wat Sopaluang.

Above: *Away from the main boulevards, Vientiane can seem more like a rural town than a capital city.*

Right: *The tiered roofs of Wat Hai Sok rise above a row of small shophouses.*

Previous pages (left): *A fruit seller heads off Fa Ngum Road towards the food stalls along the river.* ***(right):*** *Selling brushes by bicycle.*

Left and above: *Khua Din Market is the place to buy fresh vegetables and other ingredients.*

Above: Food stalls are a popular attraction in the area facing the Mekong River.

Right: French bread is as much a staple food as rice in Vientiane.

Previous spread: *The countryside is literally right on Vientiane's doorstep.*

Left and above: *Louvred window shutters remind of colonial architectural influences in the old French houses that still survive.*

43

Above: Decorative detail at Wat Kokninh on the outskirts of Vientiane.

Right: Monks walk past the ornate facade of Wat Kokninh.

Above: A woman offers alms to a monk.

Right: The daily ritual of monks receiving alms in the early morning.

Previous spread: *Beyond Vientiane, the Garden of Buddhas displays a haunting array of Buddhist and Hindu statuary.*

Left and above: *The Garden of Buddhas was privately created in the late 1950s. The images appear both fierce and serene.*

Left: *That Luang expresses an irresistible sense of serene power.*

Above: *Decorative detail at That Luang.*

Vientiane

Travel Facts

Where It Is

Vientiane lies on the Mekong River in northwestern Laos, where the river forms the border with Thailand. On the opposite bank is the northeastern Thai province of Nong Khai, with the Thai town of the same name about twenty kilometres downstream. Vientiane's geographical coordinates are 102 degrees North, 17 degrees East.

How To Get There

By Air
Most flights to Vientiane originate in Bangkok, but there are also links to Chiang Mai in Thailand as well as to cities in Vietnam, Cambodia, Burma, and China. Lao Airlines offers regional flights and numerous domestic links. Vientiane's Wattay International Airport is four kilometres northwest of the city.

By Train
There is no direct rail link to Vientiane, but travellers from Bangkok can take the overnight express service to Udon Thani or Nong Khai and then cross the border into Laos by road or ferry.

By Road
Motorists or bus passengers arriving via Nong Khai or Udon Thani can cross the Mekong River into Laos over the Thai-Lao Friendship Bridge. Vientiane is twenty kilometres from the bridge.

By Boat
It is possible to reach Vientiane via the Mekong from Huay Xai in Thailand.

When To Go

Vientiane is in the Mekong River valley and is generally hot all year round. Like its neighbour Thailand, it enjoys three seasons per year: the dry, hot season; the rainy season; and the dry, cool season (although it can still be very hot at this time of year, too).

The hot season usually lasts from March to May. The average temperature is 84 degrees Celsius, although it can reach as high as 92 degrees and as low as 74. Some rivers are unnavigable at this time.

The rainy season begins in May/June and runs until October/November. It is still hot at this time of year, with an average temperature of 82 degrees Celsius. Rivers are always navigable during these months.

The cool season lasts from November to February, when the average temperature is around 77 degrees Celsius, although there can be ten-degree fluctuations either side of this.

The peak tourist season is from December to February, which coincides with the more pleasant temperatures of the cool season. Laos' main festivals include the Lunar New Year in April, the Rocket Festival in May, and the That Luang Festival in November.

Find Out More

Comprehensive information for visitors can be found at the Lao National Tourism Administration's website **www.tourismlaos.gov.la** and also at **www.laoembassy.com** and **www.visit-laos.com**.

Above: *Girls with dried flowers at a Vientiane street market.*

Acknowledgements

The publisher would like to thank the following, whose assistance has made this book possible:

Ramita Saisuwan and Eric DiAdamo.

Authors

Martin Reeves *is a British photographer who has been based in Southeast Asia since 1990. He has travelled extensively throughout the region documenting culture, travel, and lifestyle. His work has been frequently exhibited both locally and internationally.*

John Hoskin *is an award-winning freelance travel writer who has been based in Thailand since 1979. He is the author of many highly acclaimed books on travel, art, and culture in Southeast Asia, and has had over 1,000 magazine articles published.*